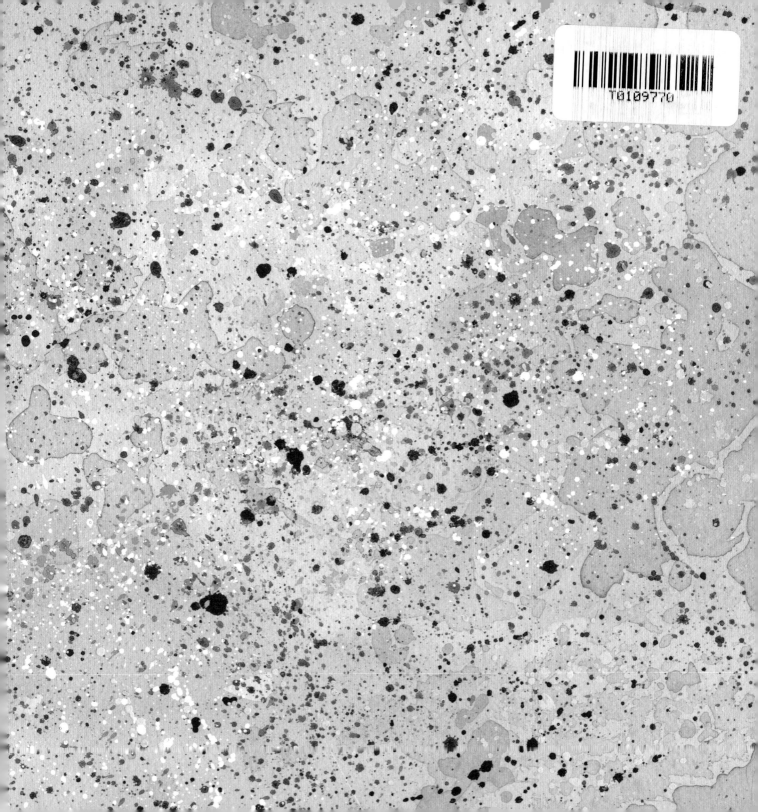

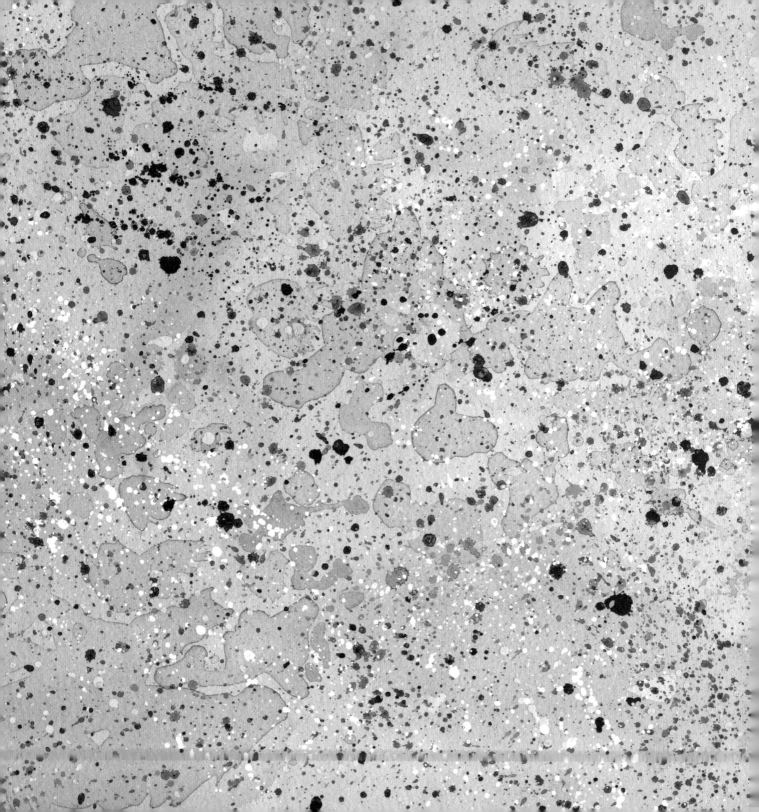

For Mia and Ada,
and for curious kids everywhere.
—LVP and TP

For Ollie.
—DS

RISE × Penguin Workshop
An imprint of Penguin Random House LLC, New York

First published in the United States of America by Rise × Penguin Workshop,
an imprint of Penguin Random House LLC, New York, 2024

Text copyright © 2024 by Lisa Varchol Perron and Jay Taylor Perron
Illustrations copyright © 2024 by David Scheirer

Visit us online at penguinrandomhouse.com.

Library of Congress Cataloging-in-Publication Data is available.

Manufactured in China

ISBN 9780593662151   10 9 8 7 6 5 4 3 2 1 HH

The text is set in Gilroy Semibold.
The art was painted with watercolor on Lanaquarelle paper and edited in Photoshop.

Edited by Cecily Kaiser
Designed by Maria Elias

ALL THE ROCKS WE LOVE

by Lisa Varchol Perron and Taylor Perron

art by David Scheirer

RISE

NEW YORK

Rocks are everywhere we look—
strewn along the shore,
nestled in the sidewalk cracks,
and on the forest floor.

A world of possibilities
is waiting on the ground.
Let's wander, wonder, and discover . . .
rocks are all around.

Rocks are good for gathering.

I hunt until I find

a pocketful of river stones—

rounded, smooth, and lined.

Rocks are excellent for stacking.

One rock, two rocks . . . ten!

I stack the flattest stone on top.

Oops! I stack again.

SHALE

Rocks are fun to plop in water—

will they sink or float?

The one with tiny holes is bobbing

like a little boat!

PUMICE

Rocks are tough enough to bang.

I take one in each hand,

then march and clap them to the beat

like cymbals in a band!

GNEISS

Rocks are packed with secret stories.

This one seems to be

a tale about the ancient creatures

swimming in the sea.

LIMESTONE WITH FOSSILS

Rocks are stellar when they sparkle.

First, I form a line.

Next, I beg the clouds to part.

Now it's time to shine!

Rocks are comforting to hold whenever I am scared.

I squeeze my rock that's cool and smooth.

It helps me feel prepared.

OBSIDIAN

Rocks are great for drawing pictures—

see my swirly style?

My palms and clothes are dusty, but . . .

my picture makes me smile!

Rocks are gifts to share with friends.

I like to give away

a burst of purple, blue, and pink

to brighten someone's day.

AGATE

Rocks are perfect climbing spots.
Up and up I go,
until I reach the tippy top
and wave to those below.

GRANITE 25

Every rock we find is different.

Every rock's just right—

the ones we've gathered, shared, and climbed,

and those we someday might.

From tiny pebbles by the stream

to mountains high above,

Earth is home to countless treasures . . .

all the rocks we love.

MORE ABOUT ROCKS

A **rock** is a solid material usually made of one or more minerals.

Rocks are grouped into three main types, depending on how they formed:

- **Sedimentary** rocks form when particles of sediment—such as sand, clay, plants, shells, or bits of other rocks—get packed together over time, or when water evaporates and leaves minerals behind.
- **Igneous** rocks form when magma (hot, liquid rock) cools and hardens.
- **Metamorphic** rocks form when existing rocks are transformed by heat or pressure.

Like the children in this book, you might enjoy playing with and collecting rocks. But it's important to ask about the rules before taking any home. Some rocks need to stay put in order to preserve the geology and ecology of an area or to respect local beliefs and practices.

Chert (Sedimentary) pages 6–7
Chert (say: *churt*) forms deep in the ocean. It sometimes has an interesting pattern or color and is worn as jewelry. Chert is often found as pebbles in rivers or on beaches.

Shale (Sedimentary) pages 8–9
Shale forms from layers of clay or silt packed together. Its thin layers split easily into flat pieces.

Pumice (Igneous) pages 10–11
Pumice (say: *PUH-miss*) forms when foamy lava cools quickly. It has pockets of air that make it float in water.

Gneiss (Metamorphic) pages 12–13
Gneiss (say: *NICE*) may sound soft because of its name, but it's one of the sturdiest rocks out there. It is commonly used in buildings and monuments.

Limestone with Fossils (Sedimentary) pages 14–15
Limestone has the word "lime" in it, but not the fruit! Lime is also the name of a white substance made by burning limestone. Because it usually forms in the ocean, limestone often contains fossils of dead sea creatures.

Mica Schist (Metamorphic) pages 16–17
Mica schist (say: *MAI-kuh SHIST*) looks like it is sprinkled with large flecks of glitter because its minerals have flat surfaces that reflect light. It's like it's made of tiny mirrors!

Obsidian (Igneous) pages 18–19
Obsidian (say: *uhb-SID-ee-uhn*) forms when gooey lava cools quickly. It is often called volcanic glass, and it was used in the past to make arrowheads and knives.

Chalk (Sedimentary) pages 20–21
Chalk is a type of limestone formed mostly from the shells of dead sea creatures. Because it is soft, it comes apart and leaves white streaks when dragged across a surface. Blackboard chalk and sidewalk chalk used to be made from the rock called chalk, but they are now commonly made from a mineral called gypsum.

Agate (forms inside other rocks) pages 22–23
Agate (say: *AG-uht*) forms when water carrying dissolved minerals seeps into holes in another rock and deposits minerals in layers that eventually fill the holes. It is known for its unique colors and patterns.

Granite (Igneous) pages 24–25
Granite is one of the most common rocks in Earth's crust. It is formed by the slow cooling of magma underground.

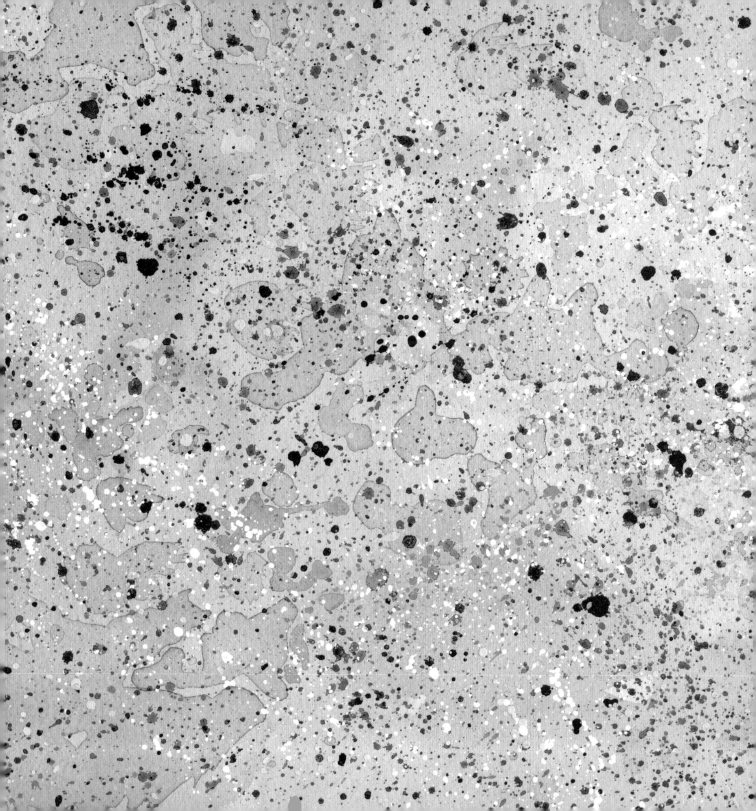

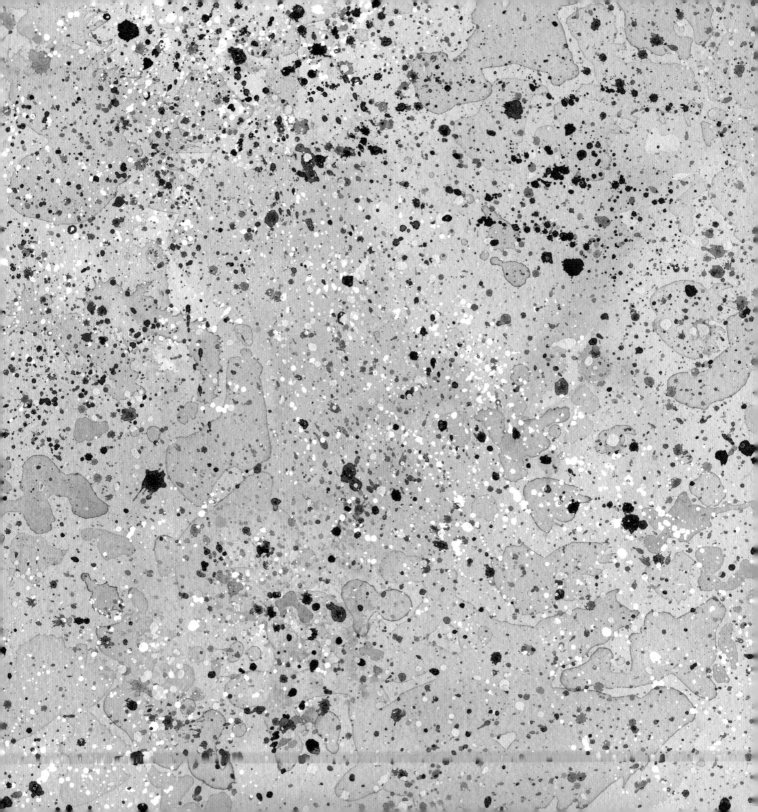